TIME

poetry **pt** today

Time And Place

Edited by Kelly Olsen

First published in Great Britain in 1998 by Poetry
Today, an imprint of
Penhaligon Page Ltd, 12 Godric Square, Maxwell Road,
Peterborough. PE2 7JJ

A Catalogue record for this book is available from the
British Library.

ISBN 1 86226 080 X

Typesetting and layout, Penhaligon Page Ltd, Wales.
Printed and bound by Forward Press Ltd, England

Foreword

Time and Place is a compilation of poetry, featuring some of our finest poets. The book gives an insight into the essence of modern living and deals with the reality of life today. We think we have created an anthology with a universal appeal.

There are many technical aspects to the writing of poetry and *Time and Place* contains free verse and examples of more structured work from a wealth of talented poets. To choose winners from the wide range of styles and forms is a most difficult task, albeit a pleasurable one. On this occasion, the winners are as follows:

G Hart	Sunflower
G Hodson	My Love for Melody
M Sutherland	A Beach in Normandy
Janet Petchey	Homesick
Janet Grice	(Poetry) In a Quiet Place

My congratulations and thanks go to them and to all of you who have contributed to *Time and Place,* and I trust you will enjoy it as much as I have.

Contents

The Poems

One Special Day
Julie Titchener

The warmth of his surroundings,
the scent of his skin,
the meaning of his existence
was known from deep within
his soft dark hair,
and his cute cheeky smile,
made being with him,
all it worth while,
the feel of his body,
so soft against mine,
kind and gentleness,
made his heart shine,
but I hope he can stay,
true to me,
that he's no heartbreaker,
like the others I see.

Ship's Log - A Passage Through Time
Davina Watson

Looking up from the dock, I thought I had never seen a ship look
finer.
I was so thrilled and excited, as I stepped aboard my first cruise
liner.

As we slipped out of harbour, these new surroundings I would have
to investigate.
Up and down the decks I went only to discover, this floating hotel
was really first rate.

By day I sunbathed on deck or swam in the pool, so cool, in
temperatures that soared.
At night I dined and danced, or watched an evening show, not ever
was I bored.

Each new port of call would fascinate and enthral me, as on and on
we sailed.
Down in the seclusion of my cabin, I would write my postcards

Then last thing at night I'd slip up on deck, just to watch the
glistening stars.
The dark peaceful ocean there below us, far away from roads and
noisy cars.

I never heard or messed the news, or even wanted to read a
newspaper.
Blissfully we sailed on, unaware of any disaster, or the latest crime
caper.

Then one day during the voyage, in the crowded restaurant, I first
saw your face.
Across the tables our eyes met, one look was all it took, and my heart
began to race.

The rest of the trip was spent in seventh heaven, somewhere on
cloud nine.
As we disembarked, I took one last look back, yes this was a time for
which I'd pine.

Now I'm no longer single, I spend my days in traffic queues and
shopping trips to Tesco.
No exotic trips, just summer at home avoiding the rain, while trying
to dine alfresco.

In the grey and cold of winter, or when the stresses of life threaten
to take hold.
I'll cast my mind back to a fine cruise liner, and smile, as happy
memories unfold.

Mist On The Horizon
Janet Childs

As I approached La Gomera
silent as the breath of fresh air
I saw mountains very high.
We drove through villages very small.
Women dressed in peasants dress
of black dress, with scarf around
their heads.
Men sowing seeds, almond flowers
in full bloom.
Oranges, banana's growing all around.
Mountains untouched by hand.
Green grass and wild flower
Everywhere.
What a beautiful sight to see.
The breathtaking scenery all around.
With lots of beautiful flowers too.
The stillness and silence of
La Gomera is wonderful to see.
Local birds singing their songs.
What a wonderful joy to hear.
I adore La Gomera.
It's beauty, silence, flowers swaying
in the breeze.
Birds singing songs of joy.
a visit for one and all.

My Favourite Place
Mary R Whillis

I've thought about this often
Of places I have been.
Have thought of castles, big and
houses small.
These have not moved me, not at all
It was when I thought I had made a choice
Of a place I really loved.
Only to be fooled once more.
It really was not so.
I thought about it - yet again.
Then without a doubt - I knew
Curled up beside my husband, my head
Upon his chest with his arms supporting me.
I know within this world of wonders
That, that is my favourite place to be.

From The Heart
Angela Dearden

My special place has no walls,
No windows or a door,
My special place is Anywhere,
Anywhere you are.

It could be in England,
Italy or Spain.
When the sun is shining,
Or in the pouring rain.

Halfway up a mountain,
Or sailing out at sea,
Sitting by the fireside,
Or underneath a tree.

For each of us there is somewhere,
That we can call our own,
But only when I am with you,
Do I call it home.

Seaside Memories
C Shanks

The seaside is my favourite place,
Where sand, and sea stretch out.
Early morning, late at night,
When no crowds lounge about.

I stroll the sand with no shoes on:
The waves caress my feet:
I call out to the lonely gulls,
Who share my daily treat.

A soothing calm I breathe in deep.
The air casts magic spell.
I cast away all worries,
And let enjoyment dwell.

Alas, it's only holidays that
I enjoy this sight:
The dancing waves that break ashore:
All fill me with delight.

Still, I can live with memory,
Of days long gone before.
When I was young, and full of joy,
Life never seems a bore.

Oldtime Dancing
E J Paget

Old time dancing is the
   Place for me
Happy laughter and talk
   with glee
Lots of friends and plenty
   to eat
It's a great place to meet
   once a week
Only a pound
   to have some fun
And dance around

Anniversary
Jago

Your Anniversary Day is here
We'll raise a glass and hail a cheer
'Twas Christmas Day at o'o clock
That you were wed in suit and frock
And on from there came five fine children
Three girls two boys and love within them
As years go by you turn and say
Just what life give us today
        Fortune, Success
But most of all happiness.
The joys you've shared from years ago
Stay memories in your hearts I know
So as you give each other a hug
And wish, and give, all your love
Don't hesitate to shed a tear
Of joy, and hope, and love, and fear
For years to come you're life you'll share
But know that you're hearts
        Will never be bare.

How We Met
Harold

When on patrol in London's Piccadilly.
Two WAAF sergeants, looking very much in the pink
Asked without feeling silly
Where they could get a quiet drink.
After directing them to a quiet pub
My pal and I went down to the underground sub.
Where we hoped to meet again
For their return home on the train.
We met as hoped, in a subway nook,
And out of course, came our notebook,
Addresses and Tel numbers we wrote,
And they took ours in a little note.
I rang next day, to make a date,
And saw her soon outside their gate,
Now we are married and content,
Now 52 years, a life well spent.

(Poetry) In A Quiet Place
Janet Grice

A poet sits pondering for a long time,
To be sure that His poem will perfectly rhyme,
Thinking of a subject of which to write,
So that his poem sounds exactly right.

Sitting alone on an emerald hill,
Everything is beautiful, everything still,
High above, a starling chirps,
In the distance, a timid red deer lurks.

Bluebells and cowslips sway in the breeze,
sun gleams through the sycamore trees,
A cool stream trickles over a ledge,
Camp fires and gay caravans over the hedge.

Finally, his poem is complete,
He rises quickly to his feet,
Runs light heartedly down the pasture,
This is His world and He is its master.

A Beach In Normandy
M Sutherland

As I walked along that lonely shore
I wanted to speak to men that had gone before
I wanted to share their hopes and pain
And I wanted them to be here again:
To here what they had to say:
About that bloody historic day
About how they fought and died on that beach
So that we could live in peace
As they waded towards their fate
Were their hearts full of love or hate
Hate for an enemy they could not see
Or love for a people they had come to free
Those brave men who went off to fight
We who are left must admire their might
And to all the men who died on that beach
All I can say is let them rest in peace.

Time

Anthony Marlow

Tick tock, tick tock, tick tock,
So goes the music of the clock.
the most precious gift that life can give
Is time, so use it now to live.

The past mistakes forget, I say.
The present is ours, now today.
The future, tomorrow will soon be today,
With children, laughter, sounds of play.

When I was young, in infant class
The time, how soon it seemed to pass.
Girlfriends, music, a teenage crush,
To me it didn't matter much.

So as your time does ebb away
Don't waste it, please is all I say!

Head Or Heart
H Green

My mind was free, amidst the
Cold and thin air,
My heart didn't know how much
It would care.
Our eyes met and we began to talk,
My head had offered to go for a
Walk.
We laughed and played like
Children in the snow,
My heart was saying yes,
My head was saying no.
I loved your smile, your humour,
And touch,
My heart and head were agreeing
Too much.
That day came quickly and I knew
We must part
My mind remembers you clearly
And there's a place in my heart.

'Mother's Tension'
Gill Ballard

I'm sitting here, it's nine o'clock,
    The house is nice and quiet,
They've all gone off too work and school,
    The house was like a riot,
I can't explain, the feeling of
    Tranquillity and peace,
The silence is pure heaven, it's
    Such a great relief.
I'm going to run a bath and
    Enjoy my time alone,
But you can bet as I lay
    There, I'll hear that bloody
        Phone.
I'm going to pull the plug,
    So I can't hear it ring
And savour this moment to
Myself, and not think about a thing,
I'm now in luxury in my bath
with scented oil's and wine,
My eyes are closed I'm somewhere
Else, this pleasure is divine.
I'm lying on a palmed soft beach
The sun is shining bright,
The blue green sea is crystal
Clear, the sand is pearly white
Oh the magic of this moment,
Oh the magic of this quiet.
Just the simple act of dreaming
Is better than a family riot.
Now I'm ready for the day.
To get on with my life
The cooking and the cleaning, too
To be a mother and a wife.

Golden Sunset
Megan Smith

Golden skyline stretching west.
The sun again is laid to rest.
Once more night falls to end the day.
To begin once more and shine we prey.
To lift our spirits and bring a smile.
Even only for a short while.
The gold and orange across the sky
Reflects on water saying its goodbye.
Shadows slowly disappear.
The sun now out of sight.
Darkness comes upon us as we retire
For the night.
A new day dawns, we wake refreshed.
Sunshine again and we are blessed.
To see again as the day goes by.
The golden sunset in the sky.

River Cree
Florence Preston

Stroll along beside the River Cree
Keep your eyes open and you might see,
The heron down the river streak
Catch a fish in its long beak,
A kingfisher with its plumage of blue
Its beady eyes watching you,
Can you hear the woodpecker tapping
And the noise of the Cree lapping,
Against the banks
Where the beavers build dams,
You might see them at play
Pulling a log this way
Swimming by a mallard duck
And a moor hen on a rock,
A Canadian goose might come your way
Maybe a mute swan is there to stay
There's a little mole
Running to safety down a hole,
A rabbit in the grass having fun
And dogs out for a run,
A squirrel darting up a tree
Wild flowers and the humming bee,
Nature's a wonderful thing to see
When walking beside the River Cree.

A Room In Waiting
G A Dunn

There is a little room at the top of the stairs,
In it you will find dolls dressed by someone that cares.
Where soldiers stand to attention with flair,
A doll dressed in green velvet with long blond hair.
Along one wall are books waiting to be read,
Fairy story's, just the thing before bed.
A shiny red train with its carriages wait,
It has to be ready, it can not be late.
There's the strains of a music box playing,
And did you hear the rocking horse neighing.
He waits very patiently to be ridden,
And will that special parcel be found, that's been hidden.
The cuddly lion, tiger, elephant and bear.
Waiting for a certain little some-one to care.
If you listen hard, I'm sure you will hear them all say,
When will this little girl come to see us,
    And hopefully stay.

Dedicated to my granddaughter Aimee.

That Special Place
Cindy Brewster

Memories of a Surrey woods
When I was just a child
A special place, a simple scene
So beautiful and wild

A carpet of bluebells
Like blue mist, rising, beyond
The dainty silver birch trees
Reflected in a woodland pond

I entered on slippered feet
I felt God's presence there
The stillness of my hearts passion
Filled me, with joy beyond compare

Suddenly! a shaft of sunlight
Had filtered through the trees
Enhancing that place of beauty
That brought me to my knees

Now over seventy I still recall
That special place of yore
The bluebells the silver birch trees
I loved and still adore

The wonder of Gods creation
The flowers, birds and bees
Will always fill me with delight
And bring me to my knees.

Where The Afton Waters Flow
Sylvia Sherriff

It's not too late to go,
    Where the Afton Waters flow.
There we'll find our love.
    There's still time my love.
Let us go - Let us go . . .

Now we both are turning grey
    And beginning to grow old.
We've worked hard on the way
    To keep the family in the fold;
And sometimes in the rush
    We find it hard to see
The love between us
    Both, Dear, you and me.

So let us go together
    With the Linnet and the lark.
We'll find the fairer weather
    And renew love's vital spark.
We'll find our old desire,
    And set the world a-fire.
Let us go to where
    The Afton Waters flow.

Where the waterfall's gush
    Breaks the evening hush,
Where the willow warblers dash
    And the kingfishers splash -
Let us go, Let us go . . .
    Where first we made our vows
We will renew them now
    By Afton Waters flow.

Where the raven and the rook
　　Play along the babbling brook,
And the dipper takes his turn
　　Among the pebbles of the burn;
Among the coolness of the fern
　　And the welcoming foxglove
There we will return
　　And renew our love.

It's not too late to go
　　Where the Afton Waters flow;
Let us go - Let us go . . .

Homesick
Janet Petchey

I want to see a Highland glen where the burns run crystal clear
And to feel the surge of love in my heart for a land I love so dear
I want to stand on a heather hill and think back years ago
'Til I see those Scottish Clansmen marching through Glen Coe.

The sound of pipes and beating drums will fill me with elation
As I make history come alive by my own imagination
I'll see the battles long since fought and watch the red blood flow
That nourished Scottish soil for thistle and heather to grow

Deep emotions will sweep o'er me and my eyes will dim with tears
As I watch those glorious highlanders ghosting thru' the years
The brilliant red of tartan will emblazon the hills like fire
And the haunting lilt of Scottish tunes will echo round the shire

As the eagle's shadow spans the Glen and the sun begins to set
I will leave the past to glory and the present to retrospect.

Silks From India

Helen Cronin

The place that gives me most pleasure of all
Is to visit our local department store.
The smell of perfume that greets you through the ever open door
Welcomes you to enter and explore.

There are silks from India, shoes from Spain.
Baskets from where it never rains,
Spices from all over the world.
And you can even have your hair curled!

There's china and glass and all things glittery,
Delicate things you can't handle;
They make you jittery.
The smell of scent gives way to coffee
Served with a smile and all frothy.

Roots
Sue Nuttall

When I was young I lived abroad,
It should have been such fun.
But I was oh so homesick,
For Great Malvern, Dad and Mum.

I cried most each and every day,
When I first got out there,
I should have been real happy,
For a child I was to bear.

The place I went was Singapore
So many cultures and thrills,
But I was only 19 years,
And I longed for the Malvern Hills

I'm back here now and here I'll stay,
I'm happy in this town,
I'll stay here till the day I die,
My roots go down, down, down.

Those Olden Times
Johns

Candles, Paraffin oil lamps then
    a gas light,
Those days of the past were not at
    Times bright,
The dark narrow streets with a small
    flickering flame,
Frightening at times perhaps looking
    for the street name,
Homes with long dark passages, maybe
    one bright room,
Those cold dark stairways, going to
    bed in the gloom,
Wooden outside toilets, newspaper in
    pieces to use,
A large galvanised bath hung on the
    wall ready for use,
An old iron mangle, with large wooden
    rollers,
Standing in the corner of the yard
    with cloth covers,
To shield it from the rains until ready
    for wash day,
When it is pulled to the boiler and then
    all hands to work no play,
The coal man with leather apron and sack
    to cover his head,
A black face, white eyes but are sometimes
    quite red,
Large bags of coal they put under the
    stairs,
Looking like large black ghouls with heavy
    boots and stares,
It is like a sound of thunder as bags are
    emptied into place,
While mother quietly counts each one with

coal dust on her face,
The house is quiet again although dusty, it
was at peace,
So with brush and shovel the flying dust
did cease,
That wonderful cast iron grate with
the coal fire aglow,
With large ovens on each side to cook
meals you know,
A black large kettle on a hook over the
fire, boiling for tea,
Also a pot on the side with a stew very
nearly ready,
How wonderful on cold winter evenings in
the fire glare,
Gathered around with chestnuts on a shovel
baking there,
With a pop and a splutter when baked and
ready to eat,
So lovely for the family as all around they
did meet,
Those pictures in the red coals of the fire
you can make,
Like a dog, a flower, maybe a house or perhaps
a snake,
In that darken room with shadows from the
fire light,
A gathering of the family on many a happy
winters night,
As you grow older, what warmth looking at
those times past,
Knowing and wishing your childhood could
have last and last.

Brother Dear
L Bale

Brother dear, I love you so,
If only I could learn to let go.
I see the errors, that you make,
And wish, I could take away the pain.
As a child, you suffered so,
If only I could have let people know.
You sought, the high life with drink and drugs,
And now your life, has come unplugged.
In front of me you now stand,
A full grown man.
Life has not been so kind,
But brother dear, I'll love you for all time.
As a child we always played,
And I long for those forgotten days.
Brother dear, I love you so,
I don't want to let go.
Stay with me brother,
And I will see, nothing else happens to thee.
I see your smile, in my dreams,
Remember us paddling in the streams.
Running, laughing, having fun,
Riding bikes and sitting in the sun.
Brother dear, I love you so,
Please stay with me,
DON'T LET GO.

Steve
M R Hay

I love you more than a Summer's day
with the warmth on my skin on the ground where I lay.
I love you more than the Winter's snow,
you glow in my heart wherever I may go.

When the spring falls I'm dreaming of you and I in a buttercup field
full of dew.
Gazing across fresh meadows till dawn,
it's like a new world has just been born.

For I want to share a seat on your rollercoaster of life,
on a journey of love without too much strife.
On the ladders you climb you may stumble and fall,
but a life without risks is no life at all.
The top may be daunting - the bottom a long way,
but don't look back on your strides or you could stray.

I may criticise, but I still idealise,
about your cheeky grin and your clever wit,
your friendly approach that's always a hit.
You're a powerful man, a sexy one too!
and I just love every minute with you.

For a minute is too short an hour is never too long,
when I'm in your arms you make me feel strong.
The strength that you give me helps me pursue,
the dreams I still carry for me and you.
But when you're too busy at work to see me,
I'll sigh and save all my love for thee.

When the Autumn has left us and the leaves have all gone,
- carol singers have sang their very last song,
- the presents are all opened and Santa's gone away;
Will you love me more than a summer's day?
Maybe then you'll be here to stay.

My Love for Melody
G Hodson

Fields of mellow, fields of green
      misty hollows - silver streams,
trees of nut brown, shimmering dew
      candle droppings, wispy air,
all remembering these things I do
      dear, constantly remember you.

Seeing things keep coming back,
      those dragonflies, the old hay stack,
the tunes they linger in my mind,
      you are the centre of it all
skipping by the willows fine
      loving still your hand in mine.

I love you so, what can I say
      you were precious then and still today.

Spring Awakens
A Dickson

Icicles hang rigid, from the eaves,
as I search for buds and tender leaves.
But, they're just not there, it's far to soon,
as I stand there hoping, in misty gloom.

Comes morning, my garden is couched in snow,
night time has dealt me, just one more blow.
As usual, this morning, I'm searching in vain,
despite my depression, I am searching again.

Hello, in the corner, is that something I see,
pushing up snowflakes, and winking at me.
Pushing the snow aside, forcing a way through,
a snowdrop, some daffodils, and a few crocus too.

Bulbs that were planted, with this time in mind,
sprouting and pouting, there are bulbs of all kinds.
A promise, that springtime is well on its way,
and a signal that winter is drifting away.

Spring is round the corner, it beckons to you,
and its a moment, when each of us knows that its true,
in that earth shattering moment, that brings us good cheer,
God sends a message, that reminds us, each year.

The message is simple, after winter comes spring,
depression is banished, seasons change everything.
Awakening spring, is a quite beautiful time,
an ideal opportunity, for me, and this rhyme.

A Safe Place
Mary Williams

The pain in my heart is aching.
To know you are going away.
But don't you worry my darling.
I will see you someday.
Your going is very painful.
But you know is for the best
You and my lovely grandchildren
Deserve all the kindness and best.

Your life will be much better.
I know you don't think so right now.
But in time when you get much stronger.
You know you did the right thing.
For you and your children my darling.
The happiness you will bring.

Untitled
L J Celik

Sinking deeper, deeper in
my aching feet uncurl,
The grime of one more frenzied day
gone in perfumed whirls.

A small haven, this warm bath
so quiet and so still.
Smells of flowers, sweet and clean
and the outside world's unreal.

I'm sliding under a scented sea,
Mermaid hair bobbing,
Listening to my watery retreat
and the city beat a distant throbbing.

In this honeyed, enchanted glow
I watch my breaths waft bubbles round.
And every flooded, clenched up pore relaxes
as dazed and dreamy, I'm borne down.

But the candle flickers, the telephone rings,
I start up, the lull has gone.
The balminess is waning as my skin pimples;
It's sheer bliss, but not for long.

My Special Place
Margaret Kinshott

My special place is in the greenhouse,
Where I have grown my plants from seed,
I can tuck myself away in the warm
And fulfil the growing need.

To reflect on fond memories
Things father used to grow,
Familiar perfumes fill the air,
I hope now, I have the flair.

It's such a lovely feeling
After planting a little seed,
To see it grow and flourish
A tree, a flower, a reed.

Paradise

John Joseph Henderson

Why shed tears for me now that I am happy,
Dry your eyes,
think of the good times we had together,
The world I lived in was stressful,
Full of hatred and sin
Crosses I carried were heavy,
So don't be sad.
The rewards I have reaped are plentiful,
To live in happiness and love, with our dear ones in paradise,
In the kingdom where I once longed and preyed for,
Yes,
Think of me in times of trouble
Speak to me about your problems,
Call out my name, don't be afraid
Let me hear you laugh the way we used to
Sit in my chair, sing the songs I once sung.
Lie in my bed in blissful peace
Look at my picture with joy in your eyes
Be gentle and kind, like I was with you
The secrets we shared together, we still have
give away my worldly belongings with a smile, for
I have no need for them here,
What I have is endless
It is I who should shed some tears for you,
I died but now I live
Prey the Lord will walk beside you, as he did with me,
follow his path as I did
And I will be waiting for you
Just a short stroll from his kingdom
Think of it, as, I have left to prepare a home for you,
In a new and wonderful place

With a life that does not know of any hurt or anger sorrow or
Sickness, wealth or greed
Time is nothing here
Just a short pause and we will be together again
Infinitely better than before
And richer in love.

Dreaming
Matthew Walker

My special place has to be,
In my dreams when I'm asleep,
As in my dreams I can go,
to places afar and years ago,

I can meet the people I once knew,
Talk to my Grandad who I loved so true,
See my friends who have sadly gone,
but in my dreams their sat in the sun,

My friends who have died,
They went so young,
So in my dreams we have lots of fun,
And I remember the things that we had done,

As you see in my dreams,
I can remember the past and relive fun scenes,
The only problem with this place,
Is the alarm goes off and I have to wake.

Sunflower
Hart

Above the fence
Head held high,
A golden sunflower
Reaches for the sky.

It turns to the sun
To help it grow.
With splendid brightness
To the world does show

A lovely big face
What power it holds,
Such delightful beauty
As the petals unfold.

Looking Back
Sue Styles

I look back over the years,
I think of my special place and fill up with tears,
It was in my father's arms as a child,
He would hold me, be gentle and mild.
The stories he told me when he was young.
My love for him, my heart just sung!
Together we would go in his lorry for a ride,
Sitting next to him I had such pride
I felt so safe and happy with my Dad.
But God took him to heaven and I feel so sad,
Although my special memory was my Dad cuddling me,
It's a shame you have togrow-up and break free
The memory of my specialplace I'll never forget.
Never to be there again is my only regret.

Cormac V Aoife
Rosanna Davis

The place is silent since you both left
No more line dancing to keep me alert
I hope you enjoyed the visit here
And will come back again most every year

The weather wasn't kind at all
So you could not get to see the pool
still the Lego Park made up for this
Your day was made you got your wish

Pity about the channel trip
Maybe next year they'll be a snip
to visit Euro Disney for a day or two
So save up your money to see you through.

Time to finish it's almost bedtime
Must get my sleep otherwise I'll whine
So goodnight you two and do sleep well,
See you next year oh hell.

In Those Hands
Helen Mathewson

Those hands that held mine
    The day we were wed,
took care of me, cherished me,
    Worked hard to see us fed.
Those hands would hold me close
    if upset, or ill I'd be,
Embrace me while dancing
    for all the world to see.
They held our new born son
    with such tender care,
The love in those hands
    only we could share,
Those hands would mend
    his broken toy.
Or swing him in the air
    with joy.
They gently wipe away his tears
    and hug away bad dreams and fears
Alas those hands are there
    no more
But memories surround me
    evermore.

My Favourite Place
I G Cosford

Egypt's a land full of magic and mystery
    Full of ancient sites and years of history.
Hot, romantic, interesting - it draws me back again
    Other places in the world are just not the same.
So go for yourself - soak in the past.
    Visit tombs and temples, but leave until last
The temple of Karnak, The Valley of Kings,
    The sound and light show, and as the voice rings
Out over this very special place
    You will wonder in awe at this ancient race.

Don't Go
Alice Devita

Why do people go away,
And leave their land behind,
The beauty of the mountains,
They will never find,
In any other place they go,
Wishing they were here,
roaming free amongst the hills,
With the wild deer,
Then one day they will return,
Regretting every day,
That they had gone away.

You
Susanna Zaliskyj

My thoughts are of you
A free spirit you call yourself
Not wanting anyone inside your
head
Not that I want to be there.
The warmest smile
That strong hug that envelopes
Your body around mine, making
Me feel good, and secure and
loved.
Your big hand holding firm to
my small one.
The longest passionate kiss,
That always seems to go
further than this
All of these things I miss
When I'm on my own.

Golden Leaves
Julie Petworth

The wind blow through the branches of the trees
Violently, so that one by one the leaves.
Fall golden brown to the ground.
Conkers lay in the grass waiting to be found.
Children run through the grass crunching the leaves
And once again the wind blows through the
                              branches of the trees.

A Summer Place
Marilynne Connolly

Listen, a plane growling overhead,
Making for a summer place far away,
Where the days are long and hot and lazy.

The sea rolls over the sparkling shore,
Hissing, as it drags the pebbles, once more,
Into its cool swirls.

Dotted here and there are polished shells in pinks
and greys, and driftwood smoothed into shape
by the oceans swirling motion.

All is quiet except for the roar of the breakers.
Date palms sway idly in the humid breeze,
and insects swarm happily amongst its overripe fruit.

A Winter Treat
Helena Douglas

Feathered trees peeping through the white crisp snow,
Snowy edged rivers where the waters still flow,
Tree branches dusted with sparkling snow flakes,
Where the little red robin his home he makes,
Hills capped with snow of virgin white,
Everywhere I took it seems just right,
The crunch of snow under my feet,
That's what makes a winter treat.

Where The River Calder Flows

Alex McConnell

There's a river that I know well
Oh, the stories I could tell
Of the valley where the River Calder flows
Happy times we all spent there
With no worries, and no cares
In the valley where the River Calder flows.

The River Calder, is not wide
It's not famous, not like the Clyde
It's a little river everyone knows
And from the village of Newmains
We would all run down the lane
In the valley where the River Calder flows.

We would all climb up the hill
And we would sit up there until
It was time to watch the evening sunset glow
Then we would make our way back home
We vowed we would never roam
From the valley where the River Calder flows.

There was the big boy's dam
Where I played with John and Sam
In the valley where the River Calder flows
Happy memories still remain
Of the village called Newmains
And the valley where the River Calder flows.

The Fields
Aileen Mathieson

The fields are yellow, green and brown,
There just a mile or so from town,
With lots of haystacks lying around,
On old, but precious, fertile ground.

The farmers work all day and night,
Their combines' lights are big and bright,
The rain and wind blow out of shape,
The yellow heads of oil seed rape.

The traffic passes along the roads,
As tractors lift their heavy loads,
The crops as crossed with funny lines,
I wonder, could it be 'Aleeines'?

There's yellow stubble all around,
Piercing through the furrowed ground,
As the evening sun is sinking down,
I hear the baying of a farmyard hound.

Winter is coming on so quickly,
The holly bush is green and prickly,
Soon its berries will be glistening red,
While the ground lies empty, still and dead.

Home Sweet Home
Alison Glithro

Here I sit, on the window sill
So alone, quiet and still.
Nothing to do but stare down
Down below to the concrete ground.

So I sit and contemplate
The wall, the peeling paint,
The crack that travels round the room,
The fractured life, the desperate gloom.

I sit from sunrise to dusk fall,
Nowhere to run as every wall
Closes in, to become my suffocating cell,
No escape from this excruciating hell.

The Early Hours
V E Sherwin

What do I think of in early hour
    of the morning
I think of you my wife

I think of your life and the
way that you live it -
I think of your love and the
way that you give it
I think of your hair and the
way you wear it
I think of your smile and
the way that you share it
I think of you my love
    in the early hours

Love
Nadia Shombrot

Her body is tired and she feels a pain
What would she give to be young again
Not to be five and to be starting school
Not to be fourteen and playing the fool
Not to be seventeen and falling in love
But to be a young mother and to be giving love
To feel pride in her body and fear in her heart
To feel the new life tear her apart
To wake at dawn in a fresh clean bed
To feel in her arms a small wet head
To feel in her breasts warm tingling food
To feel in her mind a sweet sad mood
And to feel in her being, love.

Holidays Of Long Ago
J Shinn

How well I remember those days of long ago,
when off to the country for four weeks we would go.
The sun seemed to shine the live long day,
there were so many fields and places to play.
Wydnam, Summerhouse Hill and Bradford Hollow,
such trees to climb and trails to follow.

Our room at Gran's had a window to the sky
where you could lie abed and watch clouds scurry by.
We would check each day for rain or sun,
looking back it was all so much fun.
We'd be off to Weymouth for a day by the sea,
paddling all day and then home for tea.

Sunburnt backs white with camomile,
'You wouldn't listen!' said Mum with a smile.
It happened each and every year,
we would burn ourselves and shed a tear.
Those holidays with my brothers so long ago
are memories sweet and they warm me so.

My Living Room
Letitia Glover

As I sit here in my living room content as I
Can be.

The only thing for company, is my TV

My three piece suite is second-hand.

And my carpets wearing well.

The curtains on the window a story they could tell.

My standing lamps a souvenir.

That I have had for years and years.

It's standing there so stately, looking proudly and so
Tall.

it lights up my mirror, and paintings on the wall.

My fireplace is cosy, as the flames dance in the grate.

As I sit and watch my TV until it's very late.

I've no one here to tell me, what to say or what to do.

Or tell me that I should dress up, or need a new hair do

So I'm sitting with my feet up as happy as can be

And just to coin a phrase, I'm in the lap of luxury.

When You Abandoned me
Anne Conaghan

The pain was there for all to see, Oh my face and in my heart
When you abandoned me, and my life fell apart

Wretched, aching, throbbing pain, tore apart my very soul
I feel my life was all in vain, I feel but half not whole

I thought your love for me was true, although the words you would
not say
I thought our love meant more to you, but you gave it all away

I wish someone would understand, the fear I feel today
Around my heart is a tight band, which will not go away

You've told me I don't matter anymore, your loves with someone
new
You walked out and closed the door, and my heart broke in two
Can a human heart really break? And will it ever mend?
I don't know how to fake, I don't know how to pretend
I'm drowning now, engulfed in pain and cannot face the dawn
To live without you would be in vain, please don't make me carry on
I pray the end is looming near, I've nothing left to give
The end of all that I held dear has taken my will to live
Forgive me those I leave behind, who loved me in their way
I don't mean to be unkind but I just cannot stay
The loneliness is too much to bear, the grief too big to cross
The penalty too unfair, your love too great a loss

As I leave, I realise that I abandon you
Too late, too late, I am wise to the pain I've left with you

Scotland's Autumn Trees
W Barton

What a glorious sight are Scotland's Autumn Trees
Standing majestically, some loosing their leaves.
Dressed in their greens, orange and gold,
A more beautiful sight you could not behold.

Larks, Silver Birch, Beeches too,
Fluttering gently for all to view,
The rain clouds were chased far, far, away.
How the sun shone that crisp October day.

Captured forever in my minds eye,
Filled up with the beauty I wanted to cry.
No matter what happens, I can always recall,
Scotland's Autumn trees standing so tall.

The Bathroom My Solace
Agnes Porter

The pressure is on and times running out
a decisions to be made without any doubt
Where do I find it? let me think
My mind is racing, I'm on the brink
Must calm down, and see things straight
An answers' to be found before too late
What do I do? Where do I go?
To resolve this problem, yes I know
The Bathroom
The door is closed and peace is coming
The bath's in the corner, the water is running
Sliding in to this lovely place
Head on the headrest, cloth on the face
Relaxing now, nothing on the mind
Switched off totally from mankind
Where in the world would I find such peace
The worries are fading, I can release
And where did I find it? Yes I know
The Bathroom
Now I know what has to be done
Why did I fret, the battle is won
I feel as if I'm floating in air
All is well and easier to bear
Thankful that the trauma is over
The saying goes, I'm all in clover
Where did I find it? Yes I know
The Bathroom

The bath's now empty, the water has gone
There's work to be done and life to go on
So till the next time I need some solace
I'll be back where I call my palace
With its soft pile carpet and pale coloured tiles
Mirrors reflecting the warm towel piles
Where else would I find all this and more
In that small room, behind the doors
The Bathroom

You
Andrew Hunter

You came into my world
My life was gladdened.
You came just when I cried
My heart was sad and . . .

You gently touched my aching heart
You made it lighter
And every time you played your part
My world grew brighter.

And you . . . are there in everything I do
I feel . . . you're with me night and day
With you . . . all things I know I now can do
For you . . .light up my life, show me the way.

When hope was gone at night
And I was frightened,
When all was dark there was no light
My life was brightened

In silence you were always there.
Your whispers stirred me.
You answered every little prayer.
Did not desert me

And you . . . are there in everything I do
I feel . . . you're with me night and day
With you . . . all things I know I now can do
For you . . . light up my life, show me the way.

You've moved a world thru' tears
And touched humanity
And made us face a thousand fears
Through your reality.

We each reach out at last
To one another;
Respect, accept and love
Our sisters, brothers

And you . . . are there in everything we do
We feel . . . you're with us night and day
With you . . . all things we know we now can do
For you . . . light up our life, show us the way.

A Love Lost
I Wilson

My eyes they do sparkle,
My heart it does thump,
My belly's all twisted,
Cause our lives are entwined!

When fate intervenes,
You want time to stand still,
But 'Old Father Time',
He does his own will!

The lines on my face,
They tell their own story,
Been there, Done that,
But where is my glory?

The love that I've found,
Is not mine to take,
It screams at me,
That I am a fake!

To steal a few moments,
Is heaven indeed,
But is greed, greed, greed!

What of my family?
What of my friends?
With a love like this,
Will the pain ever end!

I am giving you up
But 'Oh' at what price,
Cause I'll never forget you,
For the rest of my life!

Howard Road
Poppy Ashfield

Large clock upon the wall.
Rag rug lies by the hearth.
Copper in the scullery
For our weekly bath.

The glory hole stores
Pickled fruit,
Home-made wine upon the floor.
Stone sink with one brass tap
And towel behind the door.

A dolly tub and posser sits
By the wooden mangle.
Corrugated roof was fixed
At an angle

The sitting room was neat,
With piano and music stool.
Bookcase in the corner
Sideboard by the wall.

We had three bedrooms
Like the bears,
Large, medium and small.
A linen cupboard built
For someone very tall.

Lino on the landing was
Polished till it shone.
My childhood house still there
But the family have gone.

Our Best Friend
Sandra Eaton

You went to sleep,
After we left that day,
We miss you very much
We hoped that you could stay.

But now you're in heaven
Up there so far,
We pray at night
'Twinkle Twinkle little star'.

You watch us always
We know your smiles,
That shines so brightly
Across the miles.

We hold your photo
We hold it tight,
We say your prayer
Every single night.

We send our love
We send our prayers,
You'll never be forgotten
Over the coming years.

We'll plant you a flower
You'll water it with rain,
We hope some day
We'll meet again.

Dedicated to my dad, Ashley-Gail's grandad,
Eric Lilley who died 9-1-98

Lost Bliss
Sarah Collins

Warmth carrier, beauty instructor
How I miss those loving arms.
Your beauty makes me shudder
Beauty brought solely in your charms.

I have lost those loving arms
That star is asking to stay
Of you, I'll be free from their harms
My love, I want you today.

The Evening Sun
Mandy Hunter

Sitting on a hill,
As the sun goes down,
Looking over the firth of forth,
I gaze unto the skyline,
With its blazing bands of gold,
I follow the shore-line inwards,
As the shadows begin to creep,
Over the ornate rocks,
Placed along the beach,
As I watch the last dance,
Off the sailing boats,
On the glistening bay below,
They head towards the slipway,
As the sun begins to go.

The Castle
Jean Jackson

What magnitude, this castle in the air;
amazed we can but stand and stare.
Sandstone walls sweep down with pride.
Tiny arched windows, and turrets each
side.

A grassy bank surrounds the castle now.
What of the moat?
it's disappeared some-
how.

Hidden in the shadow of this monumental
retreat, lie quaint little shops on a
cobbled street.
In bygone days there was hardly a
sound.
Now throngs of people, and traffic move
round.

Small square windows, with gifts on
display;
with a coat of arms, what does it say?
'In God we trust' I say a prayer.
for people of today who stand and stare.
In the shadow of the castle in the air.

Dreams
Robert O'Neill

There is a place where I can go when I'm down
It's the only place where I can be me
And you could be anybody
It's wherever I want to be
And I can be whatever I want to be

There's a haven where I can escape
From evil worry's
It's where I can lock myself away in warmth
A place where all you need is yourself

In this place you can not be held back
And can't be put down
And anybody can go there because everybody can
Dream.

'A Message From The Summerland'
V Rowe

One day for all, no more tomorrow's
The day will come, when our life on
      earth shall be no more,
Then, we shall see the glories of
         'The Summerland'
When we, on earth-life, close the door.

We shall shed our earthly garments,
And love again in heaven, happiness,
         and song.
Today, I feel your presence near my
         loved one,
By thought you tell me, that you still
         live on.

Shed no more tears you say, for I'm
         still around you,
I hear your voice, see things you
         often do,
Though now I'm far beyond 'The Sunset'
         I'm waiting for you,
And as I was on earth, still loving you.

Just speak to me, for I shall hear you,
'The Kiss' you send to me I will receive,
I know one day we'll be together, and
         for always
Until then, keep on loving me, and,
         believe.

A Place Called Croyde
In Devon
  Jeannie Williamson

I look with mine eyes unto the hills
From whence I feel a great peace
A calmness I feel within myself in the beauty
of this place
As I walk along this lonely beach I listen to
the sea
I hear the waves thrashing the rocks the sound entran
ces me
I hear the seagulls sailing bye squealing and
squawking with every cry
The sun goes down in the deep blue sky
Oh what a fantasy
The wind she blows across my face
My hair it flows like silken lace
This truly is a lovely place
A place called Croyde in Devon
Again the breeze it blows my cheeks
The sunset sinks behind the peaks
Oh the pleasure makes me feel so weak
This truly feels like heaven.

Mess Room Memories
R G E Castleton

Dartboard hanging on the wall
Card games round the table play
'Teas up'
there came the call
How I long for here to stay.

Fruit machines with reels spinning
Social club outings by the score
Oh what happy times, from the beginning
Soon to be lost for evermore.

Where oh where those smiling faces
Mingling crowds, voices loud
Gone to different places
Drifting aimlessly, like a cloud.

As I peer through the shattered pane
Behold the mess therein
It's sacrilege, quite insane
The perpetrators of this sin.

The faceless ones, my fate did seal
The kiss of death, this place now bears
The wound so deep, too deep to heal.
The floor so wet, with my tears.

Next Week
Judith Anne Johnson

Next week when I arrive at work,
And see your empty chair.
I'll long to hear your voice,
Feel your hot, hard stare.

Next week when you're no longer here,
There's much I'll need to know.
Could I light up your darker side,
Warm you, make you glow?

Next week when someone speaks your name,
No tears will I let fall.
The lips which you so freely kissed,
Must tremble not at all.

Next week when you have left these shores,
To start your life anew.
Know that not one moment passes,
When my thoughts are not with you.

Next week I may allow myself,
To recall some times we shared.
For often when we talked,
It seemed your soul you'd bared.

Next week when you have taken flight,
Will I count the cost?
Mourn for how things might have been,
Regret the hours lost?

Next week when all sorts of things,
Will occupy your mind.
Spare a thought and raise your glass,
To those you left behind.

3764, Elvis Presley Boulevard
M J Hills

Thousands of miles I've travelled by plane,
To reach this lovely place again.
As I gaze over the heat soaked wall,
My eyes can now see it all.
And I'm filled with contentment to the core,
I feel as though I'm home once more.
Heavy traffic may roar down the street,
The pavement be pounded by many feet.
But I'm oblivious to all, I just don't hear,
Perfect peace descends as I feel him near.
For a long while I linger and understand,
What keeps drawing me back to GRACELAND.

The Wedding Garden
Diane Cooper

In the garden a wedding is taking place
the rose is dressed in delicate white chiffon dress
her bridal bouquet a cascade of white Wisteria
with fragrance of Jasmine and Honeysuckle
the groom black Tulip dressed in his suit
the guests are rows of Pansies, shades of finery
the children are Sweetpeas in their little bonnets
their laughter are whispers on a light warm breeze
the church bells ring through Foxgloves
the gold rings are placed on a cushion of velvet green moss
the vows are exchanged and love is entwined
  by red ribbons
the Daffodils provide the music
the candle lit Magnolias, they sparkle like stars
in the night sky
Rose and Tulip they dance a waltz
into the dusk of the evening
there they curl up together and sleep through the night
refreshed for a brand new day
  As husband and wife

Leominister Rediscovered
Lilian Court

Leominster to me - the family too -
Was just a place for 'passing through'
Before we had a Motorway,
A half-way house to Ross or Hay,
Not a town to stop and view,
Just a place for 'passing through'.

For years and years that was our plan,
But speedier journeys then began,
No more was Leominister on our map,
We'd fallen for the modern trap,
Of speed and speed, and yet more speed,
To get there faster was our creed.

The years rolled by - until one day,
We said 'Enough, no Motorway',
We re-discovered Leominister town,
We bought a house, we settled down,
Here is our home and here we stay,
No passing through to Ross or Hay.

So little known it's History,
So much to learn - so much to see,
The meaning please behind these names:-
Pump Piece, The Rugg, Corn Square, The Grange,
Forbury, Priory, Bargates too,
So much to learn, so much to do.

Not just a place for passing through.

Untitled
D S Basi

For a moment my mind was free from the shackles
of life.

As I walk down this bridle path which had both sides is covered
with leaves and branches, with occasionally the suns rays breaking
through the leaves and branches and occasionally a soft wind
breaks through leaving me to sigh.

As I walk on looking at the path ahead, I see it is coming to
an end.

This time and this place to me represents what I could imagine
as a little insight into heaven.

Peace serenity and beauty are all around me, oh how I would
wish to spend the rest of my existence in such a place.

But, to see it coming to an end.

Again just before leaving the path, the suns rays broke through
the leaves and branches an then a little soothing breeze on this
scorching summers day again left me to sigh.

As I arrived at the end of the path I looked back before leaving it
I again heard the birds twittering amongst themselves. Maybe they
were saying that we often visit such a place, but for him
who is leaving the path it is an occasional thing.

Treetops
Dean Urquhart

Treetops and butterflies
Walks in the park
Watching the sun rise
Soon after dark
The stars will soon disappear
Birds start to sing
Clouds will soon reappear
Daybreak will bring.

Treetops and butterflies
Nature is here
The sound of the forest cries
It's that time of year
Listen for the mating calls
The wind and the rain
Evergreen branches fall
It's autumn again.

Treetops and butterflies
The birds and the bees
Mornings to advertise
A country to please
Grass among the flower beds
Petals full bloom
Insects rear ugly heads
Leaving no room.

Treetops and butterflies
Ice cream and sweets
For children a nice surprise
In the sweltering heats
Dogs hiding in the shade
Tails wagging fast
Buckets without a spade
In a sandpit so vast.

Treetops and butterflies
A smile and a cry
Watching the sun rise
So high in the sky
The wind forming raindrops
Which land on my face
Falling from tree tops
In my favourite place!

Someone Special
Linda Rankin

You've had a lifetime of goodbyes
I can see it written in your eyes
Do you never tire of being alone?
Do you crave someone to care when
Your tired and feeling cold
Do you miss someone to hold you and
     To kiss you goodnight
Miss having someone special in your life !
Someone to love you for what you are
Not for what they'd like you to be
Someone Special - Someone Sensual
     Someone like me !

Someone to phone you to tell you they care
Being apart is more than you can bear
Then when you meet again - you no longer refrain
Your emotions take over your heart and your mind
You feel as though your going insane
A new experience this is not a game

Longing to be in a passionate embrace
Inhibitions disappear without a trace
Feeling so deeply you can't concentrate
Someone so warm to whom you can relate

You walk around in a daze
This time you know it's not a phase
You act kind of crazy and you do not care
All you want is for your love to be there
Longing to hold - to kiss - to touch
You know of this person you can never have
                      Too much !

Heaven On Earth
Marianne J Foord

I run and jump and laugh and play
My beloved bluebells are out today

I walk with my love just we two
Enjoying the exquisite bluebell hue

I stroll and stop only to gaze
At the sun dance on the bluebell haze

I hobble now to the beauty I know
Bluebells to fill my heart aglow

In slow procession the family walks
They glance at bluebells no-one talks

The casket of ashes holding me
Is opened and scattered - I am free

The bluebells take me - a new birth
I am at peace - in Heaven on Earth

The Riverbank
Valerie Hunt

In the quiet, sunlit, solitude, along the
    riverbank I stroll,
Making up for all the upsets, our daily
    life seems to hold.

I walk with 'Shan and Perdy' and also
    Bernie and John,
Sometimes Catherine, or even Alan might
    come along.

But early in the morning, long before
    many folk arise,
It can be quite revealing, that
    sight before my eyes.

The flowers, no-one planted, seeds dropped
    I think by the birds.
The blossoms on the trees, in which
    a tiny bird might stir.

So, I thank my loving saviour, for
    all facultys I share,
To walk, to see, to hear these things,
    and breathe our precious air.

It's Not That Complicated
Stuart Michael Ramsay

Relax, enjoy the ride
It's really not that complicated
I would suggest
That there's no need for self-analysis and the pondering of stars
Because
You just are

Indeed, if I may, I would go on further to say
That there's no need to consider your destiny or fate
Because there are only two things you can be sure of;
One, your skin will always remain the colour it is
And two, one day you will die

So, when you consider life with all its comedy and disease
Don't consider too hard
Because
Life just is.

My Place

Lemanie Kelly

I've got a place, that I go
and I'm sure no one knows
that I go there to disappear
to run away, from here
Into my lonely deepened soul
I tend to subconsciously lull
I love my secluded place
my time I slowly waste
there are no orders there
my mind, I do not tear
surrounded by empty thoughts
peacefulness is happily caught.

My Garden
Margaret Patterson

My soul may be in turmoil
And darkness may abound,
But a blue-tit comes to tell me
Of the Father's love profound.

The blue-tit is a bearer
Of God's love so dear and true,
As it splashes in and out
The water, clear and blue.

The blue-tit is a present
From God himself to-day,
To remind me of His presence,
In a very special way.

God, the great creator,
Cares for me each day.
How can I doubt His presence,
When the blue-tit came to-say:

'I'm a messanger from God above,
To tell you of His care.
Do not fear or be afraid.
He's with you everywhere'.

Sheltered Housing
Provost Hogg Court
Betty Greig

As I stand here watching the clouds go by;
Motor cars passing. Birds in the sky.
Trees which are bare waiting for spring
everyone wondering what tomorrow will bring.

Ships in the harbour pass in and out.
Every now and then a seagull will shout.
The cranes keep on moving the dockers work all day.
To empty the cargoes and let the ships get away.

I look out over the city of my town Aberdeen
It's the cleanest of places that I've ever seen
the high-rise flats gleaming so tall and white
looking from here it's a beautiful sight.

A Walk In The Countryside
E Smith

The country side is a sight to see
With rugged pathway's, and the occasional tree,
With wild life in abundance it's a great reality.
A steady stroll gives you the utmost pleasure
With God's greatest gift you'll always treasure,
A babbling brook maybe you'll see.
The sound of the cuckoo from a distant tree,
Wild flower's all around their petals tipped with dew,
Bluebell's like a carpet such a pretty blue,
The sun's rays shine down on everything you see,
Bird's tend their young as they fly from tree to tree,
When the day is over and the sun is ready to set,
With peace in your heart you will never forget.

Memory Park
Bill Grint

I walk through the park where we used to stroll,
Heart-saddened, thinking of you,
And the rain is falling
Pitter-pat, pitter-pat!

I see the bench where we would sit
So close, and talk of love,
And the rain is falling
Pitter-pat, pitter-pat!

Passing the gates through which you walked
To meet another, I feel the tears,
And the rain is falling
Pitter-pat, pitter-pat.

Today, the flowers are bright in the sun's hot glow,
But in my heart the clouds are black,
And the rain is falling
Pitter-patter, pitter-patter, pitter-pat!

A Summer Place
Linda Jacobs

Send me one more summer
Like those I used to know
Days to spend in endless sunshine
Our hearts always aglow
Strong devotion to each other
We swore we never would part
Stolen kisses
Lost in moments
But I still hold you deep in my heart
Hideaway homes built on the hillside
Where down on grassy carpets we'd lie
Secure and trusting to each other
But little knowing how soon
We'd kiss those hours goodbye
So send me one more summer
Like those I used to know
And send him back to me again
This time I won't let him go.

Baby Jordan
Dorothy Bigham

On the 6th of September, in early morn,
To Gail and Brian a son was born.
So small, so perfect, oh what joy
Was brought to heart's by this baby boy.

Joy turned to sorrow before night fell
As we were told he was far from well.
Our whole world just fell apart.
The problem was his little heart.

Rushed up to Glasgow into Yorkhill
Where doctors and surgeons used their skill
Where dedicated nurses too
Cared for this little one in ITU.

Thanks to them he fought and won
The fight for life that had began
The minute he was born.

To God who answered every prayer.
Always listening, always there.
We give our thanks for all the joy
This tiny healthy baby boy
Has brought to all our hearts.

Comfort Me
Janet Roscoe

Heartache and pain I long to share,
With someone close that doesn't care.
He sometimes see's me sit and cry,
And never seem's to ask me why,
The one that's close doesn't know,
Just how much I love him so.
That is why I sit and cry.
And wipe the tears from my eyes.
Special moments you never /
Belong to someone so very dear.
In my heart and in my soul.
Precious moments never to be told
Comfort me while I go to sleep.
For in the morning you shall weep.
You see me lying in my bed.
Not knowing I, am really dead.
You see me lying cold and still.
Because in my heart I was very ill.
Bury me beside your dad.
For I know that he would be glad.

Forget Me Not
S V Baylis

We made a date and arranged to meet
You took me to a restaurant and pulled out my seat
Pristine white linen covered the tables
Coloured carnations in little crystal vases
Silver cutlery and fine white china
Forget-me-nots adorning the edges
The waiter came, from the menu we ordered
The food the wine, all was glorious
We ate we drank whilst the music played
We talked we laughed until it was time to pay
I hoped we might do it again someday
But you were married and I was too
To do it again would be taboo
I wanted to say I love you
And you to say you loved me too
But alas it was not to be
Eternally together you and me

My Dad And Me
Laszlo Clements

There where the stream ends
The isle where the river bends,
That's where we'll be
My Dad and me.

And down in the town
At the pub, there's a round
For my Dad and me
They all come and see.

There by the hedgerow
A heartbeat away from a rainbow,
That's where we'll be
My Dad and me.

Far from the bustle
Away from the hustle,
That's where we'll stay,
If only we may.

There where the lark sings
The best of what summer brings,
That's where we'll be
My Dad and me.

The greenest of fields
Where love never yields.
Up Stoney Hill, lost in the woods,
That's where we'll be,
My Dad and me.

Our Secret Place
J M Stevens

As I walk through the gates
My hearts filled with joy,
For this place means so much
To this once small tomboy.
The headstones all written
With what's in people's hearts.
The sadness portrayed
From being torn apart.

My Grandad is buried
With my Nan by his side,
At the place where he worked
With such love and great pride.
But to me I see this place
Through the eyes of a child,
And a man who cared
About the birds in the wild.

As I walked to his hut
I would here him say,
'Don't make too much noise
They'll all fly away'.
He would show me their nests
If I promised not to tell
Where they laid all their eggs,
I'd see squirrels as well

He'd lift me up high
To sit on his bike
As we locked up the gates
We'd whisper good night.
Now my Dad laid there too,
But I've memories on my side
Of a place as a child
I would run I would hide.

And I thank you Grandad
For the secrets that I keep,
Because I know you're still there,
You've just fallen asleep.

Love Grows
G M Catlin

I've never known a love so deep
a love so deep it makes me weep
it started out as something light
and grew and grew each day and night
it's like a flower that unfolds
a lot more precious than pure gold
when two love's like ours entwine
it's from the heart both yours and mine
for all the love and thing's we've shared
it shows how much we really care
and treasured thoughts both yours and mine
will stay with us till the end of time
I hope my darling we can stay
friends for all time come what may
that you chose me to share your love
I thank the powers from above
you gave to me something so right
you turned my darkness into light
your always there you understand
when I reach out and need a hand
I'll treasure our love till the end of time
and thank the Lord that you are mine
your love that is so freely given
gives me one more reason to go on living.

A Very Near Thing
Edna Davies

We know too well how we went through hell
In the war, when we stood alone
With no one behind us
To comfort and guide us
Save the greatest leader we've known.
On whose shoulders, broad and wide
Rested our hopes, our lives, our pride.
Great faith in him was shown.

Thank God for our channel that kept them at bay,
Only twenty miles away.
Who . . . with their massive strength and mighty power
watched our coastliness hour by hour -
Just twenty miles away.

Then God in His mercy stretched out His hand
To our aid, as He's done before,
When out of the mists sailed enormous ships
Which tried to reach our shore.

When danger threatened our beautiful land
We stood man to man, as one.
'Till danger past - peace at last -
Amen - 'Thy Will be done' . . .

The Bay
Jacklyn Traynor

A million diamonds sparkling white
On the bay in the morning light

Dancing about, starlike and bright
Flickering, shimmering a beautiful sight.

A boat passes by and breaks up the dance
But the lights sparkle on when given the chance.

This wonderful view is a sight to behold
And far more precious than silver and gold.

Thank God for his gift to be able to see
And remember forever in my memory.

Your Best Friend
A Miller

Friendship is a togetherness with understanding and trust as well
Your best kept secrets you can confide, your friend will never tell
She will tell you when she thinks you are wrong in a way which
never offends
And although you agree to disagree, you remain the best of friends

When troubles come as they will and you are filled with fear
Your friend will stand beside you and help you wipe your tear
Happy days and sad days you have shared with each other
Have you got a friend like this ? it may even be your Mother

Bute Park
Ray Lewis

Five squirrels, six, seven,
Would there be eight?
I sat down quietly
Watchful, to patiently wait.

Two bounding along
Nose to bushy tail
Like one animal undulating
Leaving but a single trail.

One sat on its haunches
Watching me watching him,
Did he study us often
Or was this just a whim?

Two were picking through some leaves,
Acorns stuffed into their cheeks,
Then darted away to hide their hoard
To feed on in harsh winter weeks.

The final pair went scampering
Spiralling high up an aged tree,
Corkscrewing up to its branches
They were lost to sight from me.

What a magnificent park to live in,
Plants and berries of every hue,
Conker trees and chestnuts, and
Weeping willows by the river grew.

Neat grasses, floral garden beds,
Sunlight threading through the leaves,
I sat luxuriating in the warmth
Enjoying the gentle morning breeze.

The River Taff was running sluggish,
A seagull looked with expectant eye,
An angler stood in mid river,
He looked just as content as I.

He occasionally gave a flick of a wrist
And his line snaked through the air,
He never stirred once from that spot,
Well, not as long as I was there.

Mud near the banks lay glistening,
Exposed to the suns warming rays,
Too few people yet to mar the peace
Of the park on this September day.

'Mountsfield Park'
Jasmine Bates

You said you were feeling sad and blue,
you were going for a walk.
I said that I would come along too;
perhaps you would like to talk.

We headed towards 'Mountsfield Park',
the sky was a brilliant blue, there was
nobody else around, only me and you.

We found a park seat on top of the hill,
looking out across a magnificent view.
I laid against your outstretched arm,
and gazed out on the open space, I felt
so secure in this beautiful place, alone
with you.

It was then you turned and looked in my
eyes, and then your lips met mine.
The thrill, the excitement of that kiss
sent trembling down my spine.

The nearness of your warm embrace,
the soft whispers and kisses on my face,
is something that lingers in my mind.

Sadly our love was never to be,
but I'll never forget that place,
Where my first experience of love took place,
the park seat in 'Mountsfield Park'.

No Regrets
Margeret Upson

At night my heart cries only for you
In your arms I long to lay like I use to,
There's only a cold empty space where you laid
The scent of your aftershave now has fade,
I really don't know what brought us to part
What ever it is it has torn my heart,
Tears can be dried or wiped away
But a lonely heart is now here to stay,

There's another new moon rising overhead
He can tell the words that were never said,
As I looked up to him my tears he could see
Oh dear moon if only you could bring him to me,
They say time mends almost anything
I'll wait and see what time will bring,
time up to yet brought sadness and tears too
Will it bring no regrets and me back to you.

To Future Occupants
P D Lester

As I built 'Innisfree' I did my best,
To make it different from the rest,
A place of joy, where hearts beat true,
To live in peace and enhance virtue.
As I laid each brick and nailed each nail.
I prayed these things would never fail,
To live on inside when I passed on,
To God knows where, oblivion?

So now within these walls you live,
May they joy and love and pleasure give,
But should bad ways this house befall

I'll come back:- And Haunt You All.

Only Here For A Day
Jean Carter

Today down memory lane I saw
The little white cottage with stable door
I could see the old donkey, rabbits and hens
And hear the rook calling, again and again.

> I see the dear lady who brought me such joy
> And magical moments when I was a boy
> We'd go down the wood and pick twigs for the fire
> And listen enthralled to the songbirds choir.

This dear old lady lived all alone
And some would call her a silly old crone.
She had thin lips and a squint in one eye
But oh - she made the most wonderful pie.

> I'd sit by her knee and stories she told
> Of when she was a girl in days of old.
> She liked a Cheroot and a measure of gin
> To be happy she'd say, is not a sin.

With a twirl of her skirts she'd dance a fine jig
And if anyone frowned she gave not a fig.
To those with po-faces she'd just smile and say
remember - we are only here for a day.

> The only time she ever looked sad
> Was gazing at the portrait of my grandad.
> When once I felt I had lost my way
> She even taught me how to pray
> No need for fancy words she would say
> Just simply tell him about your day.

To re-live those days if only I could
And see the old lady who lived near a wood.
If ever I'm lonely or afraid
I think of the words that she would say
And go to the place where my gran is laid
And tell her about my day.

My Mother's Love
Mary M Rolfe

I stand aside, though time moves on.
Memories, thoughts of time's long gone,
Brought to heart and mind by
Word and song.
That tune, it's running across my mind,
I see again through the void of space,
My mother's gentle loving face,
She gave to childhood her love and care.
Always true, always there.
Singing to me, as I lay, burning hot
Day after day,
Her cool hands upon my brow, if
Only I could feel them now.
Those times are gone, but I live on
To dream and reminisce
With thoughts from long ago, of a
Loving song and gentle kiss.
She is with me still, though far away,
It only takes a fleeting glimpse,
A snatch of song
To bring those memories of times
For which I long.

Spirit Of The Sea
Herbert J Wallace

The mist was falling lightly
As I strolled on Plymouth Hoe
And thought of all the years gone by
When I sailed to meet the foe.

Through thickening mist I heard
The mournful cry of distant birds
'Twas seagulls flying overhead
Like spirits of the sailor's dead.

Still deep in thought I carried on
And slowly made my way back home
When with a shiver I realised
I wasn't really quite alone.

A ghostly figure of a sailor lad
Was gazing out to sea.
And as he turned to me and smiled
I realised that he was me.

To Realise
Patrick Hartigan

It's nice to watch the clouds go by
And wait to see the clear blue sky,
To see the sun shining through
To a sky that's now, ever so blue.

To feel the wind in your face
And to feel your heart beat a pace;
To feel alive and realise, how very near
    was your demise.

You watch the geese fly overhead
And realise that you're not dead.
When you feel that now, you still belong,
You ask your God to make you strong.

When you realise your loved one's grieve
You thank your God for your reprieve.
You feel so lucky and amazed
That you have gained those extra days.

When you realise it's time to go,
Just let us hope it's not too slow.
You sit here now and feel so great,
It's not your time for the Golden Gate!

So let us hope you made amends
And spent more time with your dear friends.
Good-bye dear Earth, you'll say with a sigh
It's time to reach for that clear blue sky.

But the day will come when you must go,
So let us hope, it's a decade . . . or so.

In Camden Town
Francis Harcourt

I weep tears on your breasts
In Camden Town
Sob with guilt, unhappiness
In Camden Town
The passing lorries make
The dusty windows shake
I feel my heart will break
In Camden Town.

I beg you for comfort
In Camden Town
First I'm not up for it
In Camden Town
Then your fair bower
Opens, like a flower
And I gain new power
In Camden Town.

I touch your soft centre
In Camden Town
So yielding to enter
In Camden Town
I dry your breasts with kisses
Oh what solace this is!
You meet *all* my wishes
In Camden Town.

Untitled
C A Moss

Come Atom Bombs obliterate,
This sprawling town
We know as Yate,
Come fireball come destroy,
Every man, woman, girl and boy.
Yate born of planners cancerous womb;
Let the radiating dust
Be your eternal tomb.

Cliff Walk To Cwmtydu
Barbara Cassini

I leave the drumbeat of the village; the rabble,
Make scrabble steps where the cliff rises,
Cleft and bearded, cheek by jowl with the
Racing sky, clouds, putti at their porky best,
Whistle the faintest tunes through thistle,
Attempt to hold the gold of the unrelenting gorse,
Sea quivers, salty snailed tails, trails
Glistening. The scree beneath my football loosening;
Sky rounding on me as I slither, grasping at
Frail flowers, root and ruddy berry, their
Fungal juice lush against the flush of my cheek.
In come the bombardiers, the seagulls swooping:
Who goes there to impair the nest's solitariness?
Look down: a miniature vessel, brown hand holding
The sun-hatted Lilliputians, whose screams, feigned
Fear, meet the fly-past of the guillemots, hooded
Show-offs, shadowing the green wave's spill;
White frilled underwear. The shimmering seal,
Tawny beauty, slips beneath the trembling sea.

Punch drunk I ascend the third hour. Club-footed
Now, I rise and fall; the pathway narrowing;
Edge billowing; sea swallowing, Sky is as bright
As Aladdin's lamp; marmoreal, numinous;
Mesmerising the late afternoon.
At last! the inlet of Cwmtydu! glistening
finger pointing to the cafe, where a tea-urn
Sizzles, and a round faced waitress beckons.

The Orchard
R T Collins

When I was a boy we had an orchard,
Not like the modern single-breed-of-apple ones.
They're organised and analysed and fertilised,
Sometimes even computerised!
In ours, we grew Victoria plums, egg-plums and greengages;
And damsons; swan-egg pears and Williams, and some for perry;
Blenheim apples, Gladstones, Bramleys and Black Tauntons
(specially for cider).
Many sorts of fruit but not a lot of trees.
(The stoned fruits made us puddings, jams, preserves and wines,
And 'fallers' and 'shakers' apples went to a local cider-mill
To bring back liquid gold in kind).

-And there was a clothes-line!

The pear tree by the cottage bore a rope and used-tyre swing,
And later on I learned to ride a bike,
By coasting down the gentle slope and falling off! -
Until I learned the painless trick of landing on my feet.
The flat bit along the bottom was my cricket-pitch.
I mowed and rolled, and sickled the long stuff further out,
And watched the starlings on the wet patch by the septic tank,
Lined like policemen on finger-tip search for clues,
Only they used beaks and searched for worms and grubs.
As I got older I learned to 'work' a ladder,
And climbed to the top of the big pear tree,
Where only birds and boys could reach the ripest fruit.
It was then that I found out that
Picking, 'potting', boxing the fruit and sending it to market
Earned money, which helped to pay the cottage rent.
In special years, when apples brought more money,
We bought goslings to graze and fatten up for Christmas,
And hoped the hedge-row holly bore some berries to add colour.

That orchard still exists
Though some trees have gone, and some have been replaced.
It looks uncared-for, smaller, seldom -used:-
But perhaps it hasn't got a boy.

Delia's Song
Hugh John Keer

When I come home late at night,
you're standing by the fire.
The light shines in your clear blue eyes,
and fills me with desire.
You take an interest in things I do,
and sometimes ease my mind.
It isn't hard to understand,
you're one of the loving kind.

Remember when at first we met,
we thought it wouldn't last.
Now looking back over all of those years,
that's well and truly past.
We've had our ups, we've had our downs,
how could I have been so blind.
It isn't hard to understand,
you're one of the loving kind.

And now the years have quickly flown,
the children have all gone.
Just who could say with hand on heart,
that we have raised them wrong.
I wish the time would just stand still.
I wish that I didn't mind.
It isn't hard to understand,
you're one of the loving kind.

A New Christian
Mark Campion

A wonderful place to go is church
God never left me in the lurch
I've been a Christian one whole year
I still like football and the odd beer
I'm happy now, content with my life
No sadness, no evil, no struggle or strife
I'm not a saint, I'm only a man
Doing my best now, to stick to God's plan
I once thought a church had a tower
Or a steeple
I know now what matters, is the people

Blessings
Rita Cassidy

The wonders of our world we see,
Whether it be the great sea's
Or little busy bee's
Great oaks tall or babies small.
The moon and stars by night,
The sun by day.
A rainbow through the rain, like tears
Glistening and falling from a heart of pain.
But there is a God who sees and cares
About even a little sparrow who falls,
And knows how many hairs are on your head,
And all of the tears that are shed,
From a heart of pain.
He is your shelter from a storm,
Your strength for today
Your hope for tomorrow
Taste and see that the Lord is all
He promises to be
For you and for me.

The Balcony Bar, Waterloo Station
Dave Osborne

We were eating brunch -
tasted like cardboard
or an oven glove
kept in the oven too long.
The food was on the blackboard -
the reality on our plates.
Plates full of reality
that refused to go away,
despite the mocking looks
of the waiter, hovering, waiting
merely to go home.
To serve was not his choice,
he wanted to be an astronaut -
to walk on the surfaces of
distant sparks of light
that mocked him as he
rode home on his bicycle
in the evenings.
The beauty of the stars
brought tears to his earthbound eyes,
that stained his face, that stirred a place
deep inside - he quickened his pace
and outwardly showed no trace
of the space race that raged inside.

Timeless End
Paul Britton

The clock has stopped no time to see
It's time to be, for you maybe
settle the score, lose no more
A dream he made, will the same
We'll see the sign to cross the line
See the light, before the fight

Skirt the wall, await the call
Fate will find, a path for all
The time is here, for some to fear
In truth sincere, no lies appear
No truth inside, just lies to hide
No redesign, the fool inside
From time to be, it's out to sea
No time to fall, or win the war

No time to waste, no time for haste
A different place another race

Eastcote
Anne Whitehead

It fought for PO recognition
And won the day for prime position.
(On every single letter's trip)
Note it's EASTCOTE, Pinner . . . or Ruislip!

Eastcote is not a tourist 'sight'
But it really exists - come what might !
Its central parade of shops is great
It caters for Adam and his mate.

There's a supermarket, a baker's
Post office too, shop for dressmakers,
Wonderful Woolworth's, Pisces fish shop,
Mad Hatter's tea-shop in which to drop.

Eastcote house 'unsafe for the public'
In sixty-four was demolished quick!
The grounds remain for all to walk through
There's still the walled garden, dovecote too.

There's now no cinema to enter
But Eastcote's still a good town centre
The lights at Christmas are just first-rate
Endorsing the view that Eastcote's great !

'Iceland'

Andrew Clough

Dressed in mystery, upon Atlantis thrown,
Legends from history held dear in every zone.
Like a siren - draws me to its charm,
As a fire - keeps me feeling warm.
A need to go there, answer distant calls,
A wish to cross where pouring water falls.
Spit-fire mountains offset the paradise,
Impatient, seething fountains underground soft entice.
A language spoken with a conscious pride -
Thru' the ages - new words kept aside.
Out to the inside, where once the outlaws preyed
On lonely riders by-'cross bare rock the bodies lay.
The tales of trolls that dwell deep in the shadows, free,
The fairies cast their spell, choose who they trust . . . to see.
Such savage battles fought from independent need,
Where blood-stained land was bought, of faith, and constant greed.
The ones who stood alone to save where 'just' belongs -
Immortalised in stone - their quests in many songs.
At last, the freedom came, kept strong up to this day,
Where faiths - of every name - live close, and share the way.
The coastline settlers afford a vital trade;
Trawling the oceans' wares, for success must be made.
While others work the soil, watch sheep light grazing by . . .
A life of ardent toil; plough fields and pray to sky.
The crystal ice slow glides along the glacial streams,
Wild valley grass subsides in winds . . . of all extremes.
See scattered lavafields, spy birds in high cliff sides,
Retire to 'Blue Lagoon', relaxed in cleansing tides.
Such ingenuity with Geothermal water heat,
Released to all the homes, some buildings, works a treat!
The crime rate almost nil, where each know all the rest,
Fish ate to overkill, fresh water drinking best.
A Friday night of fun, somewhere to stop and meet,
The young to feel as one, fast-talking in the street.
See poets all around, not hard to reason why,

In picturesque surround . . . their 'sparks' are apt to fly.
Just touched the surface here, more wonders left untold,
I'm finding - ever near - my way into the cold.
This plot - my every scheme; this ground - my every base,
In thought - my every dream; all-time my every place!

My Garden
Annemarie Poole

I am in my garden everyday,
looking, thinking, passing the time away.
In Nature the colours always seem to match,
the starlings are watching for a worm to catch.
The dewdrops are sparkling on the rose-pedals,
the spiderweb, like a lace-mat is holding on to the gate-metals.
I love my garden, where I find peace,
always discovering something new, giving my life fresh lease.
I wander in the garden even in hail and rain,
forgetting my heartache and all the pain.